T0072472

The Breaking Point: A Full-Circle Journey, Workbook & Journal

Living Life beyond All the Broken Pieces

Michelle Hannah

iUniverse LLC
Bloomington

THE BREAKING POINT: A FULL-CIRCLE JOURNEY, WORKBOOK & JOURNAL
LIVING LIFE BEYOND ALL THE BROKEN PIECES

Copyright © 2014 Michelle Hannah.

All rights reserved. No part of this book may be used or reproduced by any means, graphic, electronic, or mechanical, including photocopying, recording, taping or by any information storage retrieval system without the written permission of the publisher except in the case of brief quotations embodied in critical articles and reviews.

iUniverse books may be ordered through booksellers or by contacting:

iUniverse LLC
1663 Liberty Drive
Bloomington, IN 47403
www.iuniverse.com
1-800-Authors (1-800-288-4677)

Because of the dynamic nature of the Internet, any web addresses or links contained in this book may have changed since publication and may no longer be valid. The views expressed in this work are solely those of the author and do not necessarily reflect the views of the publisher, and the publisher hereby disclaims any responsibility for them.

Any people depicted in stock imagery provided by Thinkstock are models,
and such images are being used for illustrative purposes only.
Certain stock imagery © Thinkstock.

ISBN: 978-1-4917-2166-7 (sc)
ISBN: 978-1-4917-2167-4 (e)

Library of Congress Control Number: 2014901571

Printed in the United States of America.

iUniverse rev. date: 2/17/2014

CONTENTS

ACKNOWLEDGMENTS

To my daughter, K. Hannah: You are my sweetheart and my inspiration to continue to grow and embrace patience every day! Our journey has taught me a tenderness that only a mother can share with her daughter. You are the greatest reflection of me!

To my mother, C. Hannah: Through the healing of our relationship, the foundation of each chapter was easier and more meaningful to write. As we did our work, we used most of the exercises in this book and executed the 4B principle each and every time to overcome challenges and to break through! For the first time *we* are breaking out together!

To my friend, W. Thomas: We have been through many 4B moments, and we are still standing! The storm may not pass when we want it to, but what's important is that we learn how to dance in the rain. . . .

To my clients and students: You are my inspiration and the reason why I surrender every day to my purpose.

To M.Stadelli & RBC Life family: Special thanks for your relentless mission to promote wellness to a nation that is in need of a transformation; mind, body and spirit. Together we will change the world one person at a time.

To my nutritional coach, Gigi: What can I say? You keep me healthy, and this in turn enhances my happiness. Whenever I need to get back on track, you are there! Thank you for believing in me at a time when I truly needed a health cheerleader! Even though 135 was the goal, 125 will do just fine!

To my prayer warriors: The power and peace that resulted from the prayers going up and surrounding my heart daily is an unspeakable joy. Prayer is a state of being in which rational thoughts no longer control me but where God hovers over me in and through all things.

To my God: You are my *wow*, my *help* in the *now*, and my *awakening* every day to *love*!

INTRODUCTION

Although it is assumed that the reader has read *The Breaking Point: A Full-Circle Journey*, this journal and workbook can be valuable to someone who has not read the main book. For the best results, however, it is recommended that you read the texts simultaneously.

Michelle Hannah is a certified relationship coach. She trains aspiring relationship coaches in applying the 4B principle as the foundation of their sessions. Michelle utilizes the 4B concept in personal coaching sessions, seminars, classes, and strategy sessions that enhance soft skills and help increase revenues within corporations and other organizations. Her individual clients overwhelmingly report that the 4B exercises have been effective.

After many requests for Michelle to write a workbook so that her readers could keep a journal of their thoughts, she responded by creating this powerful, self-reflective learning tool. It is a call to action in the efforts to change your life and to achieve your goals.

This journal and workbook will challenge you to tell and embrace the truth and to take actions that motivate you, answer your questions, open your soul, and inspire you to explore the possibilities in what once seemed impossible. If you are ready to face the areas that you have to break away *from* and identify what you need to break *into*, you will experience a deeper understanding of the authentic *you*.

When you dig deeper, courage will surface, and the fear that has imprisoned your freedom will no longer overcome you. You will walk through the journey of your breaking *down* and learn why it was a necessary interruption in your life. You will then decide to restructure and learn what it takes to break *through*. In the midst of breaking through, you will focus on breaking bad habits, and you will complete exercises on verbal and nonverbal communication.

One thing is for sure: if you follow all of the steps involved in breaking free, you will succeed at breaking *it*—whatever your *it* is. Once you commit to doing the work and infusing your existence with nothing but positivity, by diffusing the negativity, transformation will follow. Remaining fully present within yourself will allow God to guide you through breakups, breakdowns, and breakthroughs, and your life and purpose will ultimately be aligned.

Take the first step, and accept that the greatest gifts are those of gratitude and giving. When you give something positive, it is guaranteed to come back to you full circle. Coming back full circle to life's most important aspects is so powerful when you come back with a different state of mind and understanding. Do not rush when you use this workbook. Instead, take your time to self-reflect and to think through the exercises. The results will be well worth your patience. Remember: we have all had to experience a 4B moment. It's the purpose and outcomes that create a healthy and happy life!

CHAPTER 1

BREAKUPS

There are five categories of relationship breakups: reason, seasonal, lifetime, self, and spiritual.

We are going to look at these five categories and apply the 4B principle (**b**reakup, **b**reakdown, **b**reakthrough, **b**reakout) for each.

Reason Relationship: A reason breakup happens when the individual in your life is there to meet a need that you have expressed outwardly or inwardly. This relationship usually assists you through a difficulty; provides you with guidance and support; or aids you physically, emotionally, or spiritually on your journey. This relationship might seem like a godsend to you—and it is.

Breakup: Did the relationship meet a need that you expressed inwardly and/or outwardly?

_____

_____

_____

_____

_____

_____

B Note: *The fact that a person meets one need doesn't mean that he or she has the capacity to meet other needs in a way that warrants a long-term relationship. Accept the reason for this person's presence in your life, show gratitude, and move on.*

Breakdown: What do you need to do to restructure your life/relationships? What are the issues that you need to face?

_____

_____

_____

_____

_____

B Note: *Once you know you need to make the adjustment, the next step is determining when to execute the action required to adjust.* Hint: There is no better time than *now. Now* spelled backward is *won*—do it *now* and you have *won!*

Breakthrough: What lesson did you learn from the reason breakup? At what point did you know that you were experiencing a breakthrough?

_____

_____

_____

_____

_____

B Note: *Breaking through is usually a process. The extent to which we have overcome the fear and pain that prevent us from breaking through determines the phase we are in. Go through the process—don't skip steps—and you will have an illuminating breakthrough!*

Breakout: What was the purpose of your experience?

_____

_____

_____

_____

_____

_____

Throughout the entire workbook, you will be challenged with a B workout. It is important that once you have identified the problem and received the tools necessary to develop a plan you move on and work out!

B Workout: Take a moment, meditate, and reflect on the need that has been met by the reason breakup. Stay in that moment, feel every emotion, thank the universe for sending the person to you, and pray that God will protect and bless this person.

Seasonal Relationship: A seasonal breakup is the end of a relationship that is in your life for a season. This relationship is there to help you grow and learn. It may teach you to do something that you have never done, something you may have wanted to do but didn't because of fear.

Breakup: What did you learn from the seasonal relationship, and how did you grow?

_____

_____

_____

_____

_____

_____

Breakdown: What do you need to do to restructure? What are the issues that you need to face?

_____

_____

_____

_____

_____

Breakthrough: What lesson did you learn? At what point did you know that you were experiencing a breakthrough?

_____

_____

_____

_____

_____

Breakout: What was the purpose of your entire experience?

_____

_____

_____

_____

_____

B Workout: Write down all the people who are toxic to your health. Make a decision to divorce every individual who is toxic. Reorganize your priorities. You should be number one on your priority list. On one side of a piece of paper, write all the toxic issues that you are aware of. On the other side, write a restructure statement for each issue. Here is an example:

Issue: He/She wanted to leave, but I fought for my love and sacrificed myself to keep the relationship together.

Restructure statement: I am thankful for the lessons I learned from this relationship. I realize that the season has changed, and it's time to let go, move forward, and apply the lessons.

Appreciate the joy of the lessons you learned from the seasonal relationship, and then release it!

Lifetime Breakup: A lifetime breakup is the ending of a relationship that you can never revisit. It's the breakup that takes time, for you must heal and come to understand all the lessons that you learned from the relationship.

Breakup: Have you made up your mind never to revisit this relationship?

_____

_____

_____

_____

_____

_____

Breakdown: What do you need to do to restructure? What are the issues that you need to face?

_____

_____

_____

_____

_____

_____

Breakthrough: What lesson did you learn from the lifetime breakup? At what point did you know that you were experiencing a breakthrough?

_____

_____

_____

_____

_____

_____

Breakout: What was the purpose of the experience?

_____

_____

_____

_____

_____

_____

B Note: *The lifetime breakup is the relationship you should never revisit. It takes time to heal from this strong emotional attachment. Oftentimes this is the relationship you keep revisiting, but it continues to give you the same results. This echoes Albert Einstein's definition of insanity: "doing the same thing over and over again and expecting different results."*

B Workout: Write down all the reasons why you broke off the relationship and why you vowed never to revisit it. Ask yourself, "Did the same patterns show up every time I revisited the relationship? How can the lessons I learned from this relationship assist with future relationships?"

_____

_____

_____

_____

_____

_____

Self Relationship: A self breakup can be negative or positive. It's negative when you break away from who you really are and pretend that you are someone else for the sake of acceptance. But it's positive when you break up with the person you are right now to become the person you want to be.

Breakup: Are you trying to pretend you're someone you're not, or have you made the choice to be who you need to be?

_____

_____

_____

_____

_____

Breakdown: What do you need to do to restructure? What are the issues that you need to face?

_____

_____

_____

_____

_____

_____

Breakthrough: What lesson did you learn from the self breakup? At what point did you know that you were experiencing a breakthrough?

_____

_____

_____

_____

_____

_____

Breakout: What was the purpose of the experience?

_____

_____

_____

_____

_____

_____

B Note: *Remember that when you break up from who you truly are and pretend that you are someone else, for the sake of acceptance, this is a negative self breakup. On the other hand, when you break up from the person you are right now to become the person you need to be, this is a positive self breakup.*

B Workout: If you were introducing yourself to a stranger with the intent to provide him or her with detailed information about the true you, what would you say? Describe who you are emotionally, physically, intellectually, romantically, creatively, and spiritually. Are you enthusiastic about who you are? Is it the truth? Are you at peace with who you are? Now choose four people who are close to you, ask them to give their introductions, and compare these to your introduction. Often we project a false self onto others out of fear of judgment or a lack of confidence to share who we really are.

Spiritual Relationship: Spiritual breakups happen when your soul opens, surrenders, and embraces new perspectives through a variety of religious teachings.

Breakup: Has your soul opened up, so you can ask yourself the questions that may prove some of the things you were taught are lies?

_____

_____

_____

_____

_____

_____

B Note: *When you ask the questions, be prepared to embrace the journey that will lead you down a road of spiritual discoveries. Your truth in your past may or may not be your truth in your present or future.*

Breakdown: What do you need to do to restructure? What are the issues that you need to face?

_____

_____

_____

_____

_____

Breakthrough: What lesson did you learn from the spiritual breakup? At what point did you know that you were experiencing a breakthrough?

_____

_____

_____

_____

_____

Breakout: What was the purpose of the experience?

_____

_____

_____

_____

_____

B Workout: Lie down on the floor on your back, with your arms open as if you are about to embrace someone, and ask yourself, "What do I believe?" Now ask yourself, "What are the spiritual truths that I know?" Do not answer this question with what you have been taught or what you've heard from someone else. Instead, think about *your* truth. What brings you peace? When do you feel close to God? I promise that the answers you come up with will lead you to begin your spiritual journey.

B Note: *Sometimes there is simply silence in the moment when your answers come. They can come from an unexpected source, such as nature, a child, an uplifting TV show, or an inspirational speaker. Some of my favorite sources are* Super Soul Sunday, *T. D. Jakes, Deepak Chopra, evangelist Joel Osteen, and author Dr. Brenae Brennan.*

B Storms

B storms happen when you utilize brainstorming to detox your brain. Often we are overwhelmed with a plethora of toxic thoughts. The idea of the B storm is to begin with a topic and place it in a circle in the middle of a page. The next step is to spontaneously regurgitate all thoughts and ideas related to this topic. Once you feel that you have released everything in your brain, you are clear to self-reflect. This is an excellent method of problem solving, which will have you generating brilliant ideas, facing fear and pain, and organizing the broken pieces so that the direction toward perfect peace will be perfectly clear.

B Note: *Below are the steps of B storming. Remember: this exercise involves emotionally dumping everything onto a clean canvas. Once you finish, at least half of the page should be full.*

B Storming:

- Draw a circle in the middle of a piece of paper.
- Write the topic in the middle of the circle.
- Draw an arrow pointing away from the circle and write the thought.
- Continue to draw arrows and write thoughts until you are completely free of all your thoughts relating to the topic.

CHAPTER 2

BREAK DOWN—NOT ME

Describe the moment when you knew you were experiencing humility.

What about that moment caused you to feel embarrassed?

_____

_____

_____

_____

_____

_____

Now that you are open to a new direction, how is the new path different from your previous one?

_____

_____

_____

_____

_____

_____

Restructuring

What steps do you have to take to face the truth about your past, present, and future?

_____

_____

_____

_____

_____

Past

    1.

    2.

    3.

    4.

Present

    1.

    2.

    3.

    4.

Future

    1.

    2.

    3.

    4.

What obstacles have prevented you from making the change that you know you need to make?

_____

_____

_____

_____

_____

_____

Name four steps that you will take to restructure.

    1.

    2.

    3.

    4.

B Note: *You need to make the adjustment in your personal, professional, health, and spiritual relationships.*

Facing the Issues

What is your truth?

_____

_____

_____

_____

_____

What are the lies that you have chosen to believe?

_____

_____

_____

_____

_____

_____

Who do you trust, and why are these people worthy of your trust?

_____

_____

_____

_____

_____

_____

What is it about humility that causes you to feel humiliated?

_____

_____

_____

_____

_____

_____

Describe why you are the most important person in this world?

_____

_____

_____

_____

_____

_____

B Workout: Stand in front of the mirror and take off all your clothing—get completely naked. Open up your heart, tell the truth, and confront the lies. The mirror doesn't lie. It reflects who you are and how people see you. It takes getting naked emotionally and physically to truly embrace humility. If you cry, laugh, get angry or excited, or feel hurt or afraid, then you must work to be fully present in that moment. Whatever emotion you are feeling, bring yourself to be fully present. Allow God to speak to your heart. Embrace yourself tightly, and tell yourself the truth. At times the truth may be uncomfortable, and the lies that you have told yourself may be challenging to overcome. These lies could be statements such as "You're fat," "You're ugly," "You're unlovable," "You're not worthy," or "There's no need to change." Once you get naked and face both the lies and the truth, you will be on your way to rewriting your story. You don't have to keep telling the same story. Here is a pen—now start writing.

B Storms

Write until your heart is content.

CHAPTER 3

BREAKTHROUGHS: THEY'RE PART OF THE PROCESS

What are some of the signs that you are ready for breakthrough?

_____

_____

_____

_____

_____

_____

What are your fears? List them.

    1.

    2.

    3.

    4.

What has caused you pain? List these things.

    1.

    2.

    3.

    4.

What pain have you caused yourself or other people? List these types of pain.

1.

2.

3.

4.

What are four things that prevent you from being free and at peace?

1.

2.

3.

4.

Write four trials that you are thankful for.

1.

2.

3.

4.

How will you implement the nine steps to get past the pain and through the breakthrough phase in challenging moments? (See page 35 of *The Breaking Point: A Full-Circle Journey.*)

_____

_____

_____

_____

_____

_____

B Note: *Music is healing and brings peace in the midst of pain. It can evoke a variety of emotions, so focus on the music that lifts you up!*

Name your songs for your seven-day music medicine!

    1.

    2.

    3.

    4.

    5.

    6.

    7.

B Workout: You can organize your songs by the day of the week or mix it up, but listen to one of the songs daily, embrace it, and be fully present. This is your moment to dance, sing, and become one with the words!

 B Note: *Remember that you can replace the seven songs with another seven whenever you like. You will realize that it will tell you an intimate story about yourself if you choose to be open to change. The result is growth!*

B Storms

Write until your heart is content.

CHAPTER 4

BREAKOUT MOMENTS: WALKING WITHIN YOUR PURPOSE

Are you ready to unleash your purpose? If so, what will it take?

_____

_____

_____

_____

_____

_____

What are you passionate about?

_____

_____

_____

_____

_____

_____

B Note: *When you are passionate about something, you will do it. No matter how tired, frustrated, or sick you may feel, you will still find a way. It's a part of every cell in your body! We know that every cell has a purpose.*

Define what your freedom will reflect, now that you are walking in your purpose.

Ask yourself whether you have totally forgiven everyone that you need to. How do you know you've done this?

_____

_____

_____

_____

_____

B Note: *Forgiveness is truly for* you *first. However, it can also free the other person from guilt and pain.*

What steps will you take to start releasing guilt and pain and living your purpose?

1.

2.

3.

4.

Who are you?

_____

_____

_____

_____

_____

_____

What life test during the breakthrough phase helped confirm that you have learned the lesson?

_____

_____

_____

_____

_____

_____

Where is Wonderland for you? (See page 42 of *The Breaking Point: A Full-Circle Journey*.)

_____

_____

_____

_____

_____

_____

What are some unrealistic expectations that you apply to your relationships?

_____

_____

_____

_____

_____

_____

Describe what the phrase "happily ever after" means to you. Does your description align with your purpose? Does it reflect the two Hs—healthy and happy?

_____

_____

_____

_____

_____

_____

What storms have you been through, and what did you do to overcome them?

_____

_____

_____

_____

_____

_____

With whom do you most closely identify: Alice in Wonderland, Sleeping Beauty, or Little Red Riding Hood? (See pages 42–49 of *The Breaking Point: A Full-Circle Journey*.)

_____

_____

_____

_____

_____

_____

For males: with whom do you most closely identify, the Prince or the Wolf?

_____

_____

_____

_____

_____

What about that character inspires you to emulate him/her?

_____

_____

_____

_____

_____

What about your purpose gives you balance and peace?

_____

_____

_____

_____

_____

B Workout: Identify your purpose, develop a plan, reflect on that plan, execute the plan, and commit to touching every life you can!

B Storms

Write until your heart is content.

CHAPTER 5

BREAK IT!

What triggers your bad habits?

_____

_____

_____

_____

_____

_____

What positive affirmations will you declare to yourself?

_____

_____

_____

_____

_____

_____

What are you thankful for?

_____

_____

_____

_____

_____

_____

List four healthy steps that you can take to listen actively.

1.

2.

3.

4.

Empathy and compassion are traits that you must communicate verbally and nonverbally. How do you listen nonverbally with compassion?

_____

_____

_____

_____

_____

What compassionate things can you say to inform the speaker that you are listening?

B Note: Listening with compassion is listening without judgment. Your main objective is to relieve the speaker of suffering.

_____

_____

_____

_____

_____

B Note: *If you decide to break it, whatever it is, this will usher you into breaking free! When you make the choice to break it, you are making the choice not to consistently repeat it. If the "it" causes fear, pain, confusion, or poor health, embrace the blessing that is in the breaking!*

B Note: *Review the BREAK acronym on page 54 to assist with the next exercise.*

B Workout: Write down the habits that prevent you from being healthy and happy. Then, for every habit, list why you do it and how you expect to break it.

Explain how you practice being an unselfish listener.

I allow the speaker to …

(Suggestion: *I allow the speaker to complete his or her statements.*)

I open my heart to …

(Suggestion: *I open my heart to learn and grow.*)

I listen …

(Suggestion: *I listen without judgment as the speaker is communicating.*)

It is so important that …

(Suggestion: *It is so important that in all things we do, we respond in* love, *because when everything else fails, love will stand.*)

I respond to people with love by …

I respond to love by …

B Storms

Write until your heart is content.

CHAPTER 6

LOVE BREAKS

Reflect on some intense moments in your workplace. How do you promote love breaks in your work environment?

_____

_____

_____

_____

_____

_____

B Note: *You don't always have to announce a love break. Remember, it's the action that determines the result.*

We all have tense moments with our children sometimes. But instead of screaming or isolating, we can take a love break with them!

List four ways that you can take a love break with your children.

   1.

   2.

   3.

   4.

B Note: *Remember that when taking a love break, you cannot discuss the problem or issue you are having. This is about taking a moment and showing nothing but love in that moment. You can do something fun, show affection, play a game, and so on. I promise that when you address the issue later, things will not be as tense.*

Imagine that you are in conflict with your loved one, and it's escalating because you aren't connecting. You may be in desperate need of a love break! Come on, you *know* you love him/her.

List some creative ways you can reverse the negativity and infuse it with some love breaks.

1.

2.

3.

4.

What prevents you from taking a love break?

_____

_____

_____

_____

_____

_____

What is the cause of the breakdown in communication?

_____

_____

_____

_____

_____

_____

How will you benefit by taking love breaks in your relationship?

_____

_____

_____

_____

_____

_____

B Workout: Purchase a sexy T-shirt that has the message you want your honey to exercise—for instance, TAKE A BREAK AND LOVE ME, TAKE A BREAK AND STOP FUSSING, TAKE A BREAK AND SMILE, or PUCKER UP!

It's time to take a love break! Check out thelovebreak.com.

B Storms

Write until your heart is content.

CHAPTER 7

THIS IS TRANSFORMATION

Where do you need transformation to take place in your life?

_____

_____

_____

_____

_____

_____

List four reasons why you are ready for a radical shift.

1.

2.

3.

4.

Describe your hoodie-to-heels moment.

_____

_____

_____

_____

_____

_____

The 4B Principle of Transformation

What do you need to break away from?

_____

_____

_____

_____

_____

What needs to break down in order for you to open up your heart to learning the lessons?

_____

_____

_____

_____

_____

In order to break through, you must embrace the six steps of transformation and reflect on each one.

1. Be quiet so you can hear your inner voice.

What is your inner voice telling you? What do you need to do? How will you get there?

_____

_____

_____

_____

_____

_____

2. Forgive the past.

List the individuals you need to forgive and how you will forgive them.

_____

_____

_____

_____

_____

3. Put on positive qualities; put away negative qualities.

What are your positive qualities? How will you show them?

_____

_____

_____

_____

_____

What are your negative qualities? How will you deemphasize them?

_____

_____

_____

_____

_____

_____

4. *Surround yourself with honest support.*

Who provides you support, and how do they support you?

_____

_____

_____

_____

_____

5. *Be open to the possibility of the impossible.*

List the things that you feel are impossible.

_____

_____

_____

_____

_____

List what would need to happen in order to make these things possible.

_____

_____

_____

_____

_____

_____

6. Be patient—change takes time.

In what areas of your life do you find yourself always rushing?

_____

_____

_____

_____

_____

In what areas of your life are you the most patient?

_____

_____

_____

_____

_____

B Note, Scenario 1: *Think about how your moments of rushing and your moments of patience relate to one another. For example, are you always rushing to get to the next step in a relationship but patient when your partner's behavior is unhealthy? In this case, skipping steps will cause you to miss some very important signs pointing to unhealthy areas. In fact, the patience you have for the unhealthy behavior is actually the disappointment you have in yourself for skipping those steps!*

B Workout, Scenario 2: Think about how your moments of rushing and your moments of patience relate to one another. For example, are you always rushing to get to the bottom line with a potential client? Perhaps you are focusing too much on profit, and you don't take the time or patience to determine whether this client aligns with your goals. You are now forced to be patient while undergoing a lengthy process of approval, only to find out midway through the process that the client is not a good fit. What's the lesson here? If you had not skipped the step of evaluating the client, time would not have been wasted, and you could have spent your time on a client who needs your expertise.

To break out, you must look like and feel *transformation*.

What is your personal definition of what transformation *feels* like?

_____

_____

_____

_____

_____

_____

What is your personal definition of what transformation *looks* like?

_____

_____

_____

_____

_____

_____

Write your story of transformation. How do you want it to read?

_____

_____

_____

_____

_____

_____

This next statement will transform the way you love and receive love: "I love you in a place where there's no space or time." This line comes from "A Song for You," by Donny Hathaway. This exercise is extremely mental. Therefore, first take the time to self-reflect: have an intimate conversation with yourself about what it means to love in a place where there is no space or time. Then wait. Listen to your soul, where your truth lies. Some call it intuition. You will be on the journey that will define unconditional love. You will know when you have had a 4B moment! The evidence is the transformation that will be undeniable to you and to the world.

B Storms

Write until your heart is content.

CHAPTER 8

THE GIFT OF GIVING

Living Your Best Life—Every Moment

Write a plan of action for how you can live your best life in every moment. Think about these areas:

1. Things you are committed to (be very specific)
2. Immediate goals (be sure each goal can be measured)
3. How you will execute the plan

Don't talk about it—*B* about it!

Call up your support group and tell them your plan. These are the people who will hold you accountable for your commitments. They love and support you, and they want you to be successful and to live your best life!

The ability to practice gratitude is one of the greatest gifts you have. It allows you to focus on your blessings, on what is good and lovely. You can also show gratitude for the tests and trials that come with life. Oftentimes beautiful lessons result from the trials that you have gone through, so even the trials deserve a thank-you!

Write a list of all the trials you are thankful for. For each trial, write the lessons that you learned from it.

1.

2.

3.

4.

Practice the Gift of Giving

Giving provides an unbelievable sense of joy. You can give in the moment, on the spot. For example, complimenting someone makes a difference in his or her day—or even life.

List ways that you can spontaneously give to strangers, family members, or people who are not so nice to you (this is a huge one).

1.

2.

3.

4.

B Note: *A lifelong friend of mine, J. H., has started a tradition called Pay It Forward Friday (PIFF). He began challenging people via social media to give five dollars to a person they didn't know and post a picture of that person. He later added that people could give a compliment or a smile instead of money. This is a wonderful example of the gift of giving. Any day of the week is perfect; it's up to you. In my first book,* The Breaking Point: A Full-Circle Journey, *I spoke about how smiles and compliments change the course of someone's day, and I am a testament that it works! Giving is contagious; you will not only be a blessing but also be blessed.*

B Workout: Volunteer for an organization that touches your life, and in turn you will touch others.

Smile, smile, smile. This is a great workout for your face and your peace of mind. Trust me—it will keep you younger from the inside out.

B Storms

Write until your heart is content.

CHAPTER 9

LIVING LIFE BEYOND ALL THE BROKEN PIECES

What do you know at this moment about your health?

_____

_____

_____

_____

_____

_____

What have you learned about the relationship with yourself?

_____

_____

_____

_____

_____

_____

_____

What do you know at this moment about your romantic relationship?

_____

_____

_____

_____

_____

What do you know at this moment about your work?

_____

_____

_____

_____

_____

What do you know at this moment about your parents?

_____

_____

_____

_____

_____

_____

Who, or what, do you need to return to in order to be at peace?

_____

_____

_____

_____

_____

_____

List who, or what, you need to reconnect/disconnect in order to let go.

    1.

    2.

    3.

    4.

B Workout: Write your own love letter to God.

B Storms

Write until your heart is content.

FINAL NOTE

Now that you have reached the conclusion of this workbook and completed every exercise, you have connected to a new beginning; you have come full circle. Allow me to say congratulations on starting a great journey and opening your soul up to love. Finding your self is a process, and the necessary steps are not easy—but nothing worth doing ever is. Learning the lessons from the breakups, growing in the midst of the breakdowns, and gathering courage for the breakthroughs are the keys to true transformation.

Doing this work prepares you for your divine purpose. Your *purpose* is the reason why you exist. My hope is that the B notes and the B workouts have helped you to plan and put into action the goals, dreams, visions, and love you have within and to share them with the world. Remember that what you have learned in this book is not a completion but the launch of a healthy and balanced life. Three years after writing it, I still read my book in its entirety when I am feeling a little unbalanced. As I grow, teachings from my first book initiate different experiences. It's as if my soul opens up again and again. Thus the self-reflection and journaling that you have practiced in these exercises may look very different when you repeat them a year from now. Keeping a record of your thoughts from year to year is a powerful way to track your progress. Restructuring, meditating, and adjusting are all necessary for continued growth. Don't fight against change—embrace it. The course of action will be much easier.

My friends, please remember to be fully present in your daily lives, which means not being distracted by other things that prevent you from listening. *Listening* to others and to your inner self is the key to discovering where your truth lies. Surrender to what you resist the most, and break away from whatever prevents you from coming closer and closer to what is sacred. The definition of *sacred* is different for each of us. Sacred, to me, is a spiritual connection: love, living life, being fully present, and, most of all, my relationship with God! At some point in your life you may find yourself broken, but if you surrender to whatever has caused brokenness, you will find your personal definition of what it is to be whole!

Love,
Michelle

THE 4B PRINCIPLE AFFIRMATIONS

Breakup

I wish you nothing but peace, love, and happiness, and I release you, _____ [person's name].

The season that we have shared has brought me unexplainable joy. I realize that the season has changed, and it's time to let go.

I respect and honor who I am and who _____ [person's name] is, which results in my respecting and honoring the separation that led us in different directions.

Breaking away from _____ [person's name] has opened up many possibilities in my life.

B Note: *At first it's not easy to pray for someone who has hurt us or to release nothing but good energy toward him or her. If you do it consistently, however, you will begin to believe your words. Trust yourself, and know that if you are breaking away from something unhealthy to become healthy, you are opening yourself up to unlimited possibilities.*

Breakdown

I am open to guidance, and I commit to restructuring my life.

I have the courage to be humble.

I am able to build strong relationships through the lessons I have learned.

I embrace change and transformation.

B Note: *Experiencing a breakdown of any kind causes us to make choices. If we choose to be humble and to learn the lesson, true transformation will follow!*

Breakthrough

Every day, every moment, I am getting better and better.

I am responsible for my own spiritual, physical, and emotional growth.

I love me in the place that I am.

Through forgiveness, I release myself and others from guilt and pain.

B Note: *It takes too much energy to be angry, hurt, resentful, or hateful toward someone or something. Remember that the energy you put out circles right back to you in some way. Release it! Let go, and let love!*

Breakout

The more love I give, the more I receive.

I can meet new opportunities without fear but with courage.

I am excited about unleashing my purpose.

I am honest, and that allows me to be consistently naked and free.

B Note: *Now that you are here, take a bow! Once you identify your purpose, you have to unleash it (set it free) and be fully present in it at every moment.*

GLOSSARY

B Note—A highlighted message that aids in understanding the topic.

B Workout—An exercise that a reader engages in by executing learning and self-reflection tools and following the blueprint of a plan.

Breakdown—A sudden lapse in health and strength that causes one to cease functioning. One's purpose, occupation, close and distant relationships, physical health, and mental health come to an abrupt standstill. It is a state in which humility resides and lessons are learned.

Breakout—an emergence from being confined, restrained, or imprisoned by fear. One will know his/her purpose and reason for existing.

Breakthrough—A state in which self-examination has caused one not only to face fear and pain but also to conquer it. One will have broken down all the barriers and positioned him/herself for breakout.

Breakup—To break away from someone or something that causes a toxic environment.

Lifetime breakup—The ending of a relationship that one can never revisit. It's the breakup that takes time, for one must heal and come to understand all the lessons that were learned from the relationship.

Reason breakup—The ending of a relationship in which an individual in one's life is there to meet a need that one has expressed outwardly or inwardly.

Seasonal breakup—The ending of a relationship that is in your life for only a season. This relationship is there to help you grow and learn.

Self breakup—The process of breaking away from the negative self and embracing the positive self.

Spiritual breakup—A spiritual awakening that occurs when things one has believed about God and religion are called into question, and one is challenged to have the courage to explore one's discoveries.

The 4B Principle—A principle that defines the relationships among the four Bs: breakup, breakdown, breakthrough, and breakout.

- "I love you in a place where there's no space or time"—Loving in a place where there is no *and* or *but*; the spaces are full. Every empty space is filled by love and is not controlled by time. It supersedes the beginning (birth) and the end (death), as time is not a restraint. This place in love is unconditional, before birth and after death.

MRH ACADEMY

You can become an accredited and certified coach. This program is offered in conjunction with the Coaching Academy of North America Inc. Classes start monthly. Upon graduation, you will be a certified professional life coach, so you can start offering life-coaching services, and you can also be certified in two other areas of your choice, such as Broken Relationship Life Coach, Breakup Coach, Pre-Engagement Coach, Widow Coach, Women Empowerment Coach and Women Wellness Coach. If you are interested in the business relationship coach niche, you can choose from Business Turnaround Coach, Leadership in Ministries Coach, Sales/Relationship Marketing Coach, and Work/Life Balance Coach.

Relationship Coach

Whether you need a relationship coach or want to become a relationship coach, we can assist you on that rewarding journey. Relationship is the foundation of any connection. How one relates to another determines the temperature of the relationship and its level of success or failure. Teaching others how to maneuver through the complexities of a relationship is very rewarding; the plans that you provide for your clients will enhance and transform their relationships.

Choosing a niche can be difficult. We will provide a free consultation on the benefits and challenges of each. Our effective questionnaire will motivate you to get to the core of who you are and unleash your true passion. If you are passionate about the niche you choose, your purpose will become clearer each and every day.

Business Relationship Coach

Oftentimes when we define the word *relationship,* we assume that it is a connection between a man and a woman. However, relationship is any connection in which two people are involved. The forging of a business relationship involves making a connection, establishing trust, developing a rapport, and assessing the needs of both people.

If you are interested in seeing or becoming a certified Business Relationship Coach, we are here to aid in accomplishing that goal. When choosing a niche in this area, it is important to know that understanding the relationship is essential to the success of coaching. If the goal is to obtain a higher standard of business, it requires a stronger and deeper level of relationship. Once you understand that, you will be able to coach your clients with a step-by-step process in strengthening their relationships. Providing them with plans for identifying their core competencies and bringing value to their relationships will result in unlimited opportunities.

Resources:

www.mikellifecoaching.com

Contact Info.: info@mikellifecoaching.com or 888-983-4446

www.michellerhannah.com

www.thelovebreak.com